the swingle singers
ticket to ride
a collection of Lennon and McCartney arrangements

the swingle singers
ticket to ride
a collection of Lennon and McCartney arrangements

PUBLISHED BY

Contemporary
A Cappella
Publishing

EXCLUSIVELY DISTRIBUTED BY

HAL•LEONARD® CORPORATION

CREDITS

ISBN 0634060244

ARRANGERS

WARD SWINGLE founded the swingle singers in 1963 and has since been the group's Musical Advisor. He continues to write arrangements for the group.

JONATHAN RATHBONE, MARK WILLIAMS and BEN PARRY are former members/Musical Directors of the swingle singers and have contributed many arrangements to the group's repertoire.

CAROL CANNING and ANDREW GRAY are former members of the swingle singers.

ALEXANDER L'ESTRANGE has written many arrangements for the swingle singers and played double bass for their 40th anniversary tour in 2003.

SIMON LESLEY is a friend of the swingle singers and wrote his arrangement specially for the Ticket to Ride recording.

PRODUCTION TEAM

ALEXANDER L'ESTRANGE (producer) was the producer for "Ticket to Ride" and later "Mood Swings," the group's jazz album.

JOHN MILNER (Sound Engineer/producer) was the group's Sound Engineer for thirteen years.

JOANNA FORBES (Musical Director/co-producer) has directed and co-produced/produced four more swingle singers albums since "Ticket to Ride". She has been Musical Director since 1999.

THE BOOK

Book design by JEREMY SADLER and MEINIR THOMAS
Type-setting of arrangements by TOM BULLARD
Editing and production by DON GOODING

PUBLISHED BY

CONTEMPORARY A CAPPELLA PUBLISHING
P.O. Box 159
Southwest Harbor, ME 04679
(800) 827-2936
www.capublish.com

TABLE OF CONTENTS

Reflecting back to 1999....

It was certainly an exciting year. For all eight of us, this was our first swingle singers recording; the last time this had happened was in 1963 with the group's debut recording: 'Jazz Sébastien Bach'! the swingle singers had been planning to make a Beatles album for years - many of the arrangements were already popular among audiences around the world – and this seemed like the perfect time to do it. We were young, new to the group, with a lot of energy and ideas and the arrangements gave us scope to use our collective imagination. It felt like the beginning of a new era and so, when Alexander L'Estrange wrote us his stunning arrangement of *Ticket to Ride*, I thought "Yes, there's our title!"

Making the album....

When the swingle singers and The Beatles hit the big time in the 1960s it was because they were each doing something that the world had never heard before. With 'Ticket to Ride' I was keen for us to create something new by experimenting in the studio and exploring the potential of each arrangement, whilst at the same time retaining that special sound which is still unmistakably the swingle singers. We were lucky enough to be working with Dr. John Milner, who had been the sound engineer with the group for ten years, and Alexander L'Estrange, producer and musician extraordinaire.

Although the arrangements work very well for non-amplified choirs, one of the advantages of being an amplified group is that there are all sorts of special sound effects at our disposal. For *Birthday* we enjoyed enhancing the sound of the electric guitars with distortion; for *Ticket to Ride* and *Revolution* we used tape delay which instantly evokes the sound of John Lennon's voice. The penultimate song on the album, Jonathan Rathbone's version of *I am the Walrus*, presented us with the ideal opportunity to have some fun; Jes Sadler (baritone) organised for each singer to come to the microphone for just one minute and let their imagination run.... By merging the various bits and playing with different levels of reverberation we managed to create something suitably psychedelic for the end of the track!

Just as we came to the end of our recording period, I was chatting to former Musical Director, Mark Williams, who mentioned that he had always intended to write an arrangement of *Goodnight*. I thought that this would make a great ending to the album and so he completed it and faxed it through to us! We recorded it two days later and it has since become a favourite final encore piece the world over.

If we didn't know each other very well before we started recording, we certainly did by the time we finished! It simply isn't possible to have inhibitions when you're standing opposite someone in a small space making car noises at each other!

One of the things I like most about this collection of arrangements is the wonderful variety of approaches to the original songs. Some, for example Ward's version of *When I'm 64*, stay very close to the original; others, for example Jonathan's *All My Loving*, create a completely new piece. The wide range of styles is partly due to the number of different arrangers who contributed. We are very proud of our 40-year heritage and it's great to be able to collect together the work of arrangers spanning those forty years.

How the Book came about....

Since the release of the CD, we have been inundated with requests from choirs and a cappella groups who want to perform our Beatles arrangements. The new songs, such as Simon Lesley's *Drive My Car*, have become as popular as classics such as Jonathan Rathbone's *The Fool on the Hill* and have formed an integral part of our performing repertoire over the years. So, when Don Gooding, of Contemporary A Cappella Publishing, showed an interest in publishing the arrangements we jumped at the chance. Some of you, in your keenness to start performing the pieces, have even had a go at transcribing the songs from the CD! Thank you for sending those to us.

We have included Jonathan Rathbone's version of *Here, There and Everywhere* as a "bonus song" in this collection. We know that many of you will appreciate the chance to perform this lovely arrangement, even though we decided not to include it on the CD.

Thank you....

To all our fans... a huge thank you for your loyal support and encouragement over the years. Thank you also for your patience as you've waited for these songs to be published. We hope that you will enjoy the chance to sing these superb arrangements at last and that they may become as important a part of your group's repertoire as they have become for us. Visit us at www.swinglesingers.com and let us know how you get on! We hope to see you soon.

On behalf of the swingle singers,
very best wishes from
Joanna Forbes

It may seem strange for a group founded on Bach to record The Beatles. In fact, it's about time. As well as giving us some of the world's most popular and enduring songs, Lennon and McCartney, together with Harrison, Starr and Martin, broke down the barriers of jazz, classical and popular music through innovation and experimentation. Sound familiar?

In the early Sixties the swingle singers were wowing live audiences worldwide with the sound of 'Jazz Sébastien Bach.' Meanwhile The Beatles "began to convey on record the impact achievable live by an amplified group." So writes Ian MacDonald in his Beatles bible, <u>Revolution in the Head</u>. The track he is referring to is *Ticket to Ride*, a chiming lament with a massive sound for its time. Flouting songwriting convention and ignoring the assumed limitations of recording technology, *Ticket to Ride* marks the beginning of their most prolific and significant period. No one in popular music has produced work of such value, of such influence. And in all music? We may have to go all the way back to Bach…

For a long time a cherished part of our live programme, these treasures are from Lennon and McCartney's richest seam of songwriting. Be they literal interpretation, cool jazz or dreamy psychedelia, all the tracks are created using the human voice (or body) and are suffused with that unique 'swingle sound.'

In the early days of the group, Ward Swingle found that Bach's music was known everywhere, giving the swingle singers a 'built-in audience.' Established classics such as *Yesterday* or *When I'm Sixty-Four* now prompt the same instant recognition. Ward said a little later: "Whatever music we take, we'll try to show it the same respect that I believe we showed Bach." We hope you think we have done so with these Beatles songs. After all, you – the audience – are always our 'Ticket to Ride.'

Jeremy Sadler, 1999
Taken from the sleeve notes to the original CD release of 'Ticket to Ride'.

We are very grateful to Ward Swingle for his permission to use the following excerpts from his book Swingle Singing. In the book, he tells the story of both the French and English groups, his own story, and defines Swingle Singing techniques with illustrations from his arrangements and compositions.

How the group began....

'the swingle singers began as a vocal exercise by a group of freelance session singers working in Paris in the early sixties. Most of our studio singing was limited to background vocals - oo's and ah's behind people like Charles Asnavour and Edith Piaf. Sometimes Michel Legrand, who was just beginning to make a name for himself, gave us some fine jazz vocal things to do. But Michel went off the Hollywood to compose film scores, and with the arrival of rock and pop music the vocal arrangements became boringly simple; we began looking around for meatier musical nourishment. I got out Bach's "Well-Tempered Clavichord" and we began reading through the preludes and fugues just to see if they were singable. We soon found, like many before us, that we were swinging Bach's music quite naturally. Since there were no words, we improvised a kind of scat singing à la Louis Armstrong, which we later reduced to simple doo's and boo's, dah's and bah's so as not to get in the way of Bach's counterpoint.

Jazz Sebastien Bach...

We continued rehearsing in our off time and then approached Philips about making a recording. We thought we might sell a few records to our families and friends. As a matter of fact, in France that's about what happened. Fortunately, when the recording came out in the States (in 1963), there were a few disk-jockeys who liked it and who spread the word. It began climbing the charts, eventually making the top 10, then staying in the top 100 for almost a year and a half. That first recording, and the two that followed it, won Grammies for "Best Performance by a Chorus." The first Bach's Greatest Hits (Jazz Sébastien Bach in France) also won a Grammy for "Best New Artist."

What is "Swingle-singing"?....

Swingle-singing is best described as the use of the voice as an instrument in a fusion of jazz and classical styles. In a sense, one leads to the other. Once the singer masters the skips and jumps of the instrumental writing, the jazz feeling follows instinctively, as does the scat-singing. In fact, until I began publishing my arrangements in printed form, I never wrote the scat syllables down. The singers could improvise better scat than I could write. Of course, Bach is the most swinging of all baroque composers: with his music you can shift easily from a baroque to a jazz style by simply altering the rhythmic inflections.

A labour of love...

The most satisfying aspect of the whole swingle singers experience is the fact that it began as a labour of love. Even had it not been commercially successful, I think that the people who took part would still remember it as a special event in their lives. I like to believe that there was a nice conjuncture of time, place and people that made the original group happen. '

    From Swingle Singing by Ward Swingle

    For more information and details of how to obtain the book, go to www.wardswingle.com

And finally, from Ward.....

"The current line-up of singers, under the expert guidance of music director Joanna Forbes, is one of the best ever. Confident that they can meet new challenges and create new horizons, these singers are poised and ready for the next forty years."

EDITOR'S NOTES

By Joanna Forbes & Tom Bullard

SCAT: The scat syllables printed are the ones we use on the CD, but we would encourage you to experiment with different syllables in order to find sounds that work well for your group. Our low bass often sings on 'dm' to imitate the sound of the double bass. However, you may find that this doesn't project enough for the rest of the voice parts to be able to hear it. Again, experiment until you find a satisfactory solution.

STRUCTURE: Some of our arrangements end with a long fade-out which can be difficult to reproduce acoustically. In some cases, we have altered the ending to make it more appropriate for a performance by a choir. We haven't even attempted to reproduce exactly the ending of *I Am The Walrus*!

PERCUSSION: Vocal drumming is more effective on close microphone than acoustic. You may prefer to leave it out altogether. However, it is an art which is becoming increasingly popular and we hope that vocal percussion enthusiasts will have a go at challenges such as the drum part in *Drive My Car*. You may also notice that we added extra percussion parts on the CD in *Revolution* and *Day Tripper* which aren't in the original arrangements, so do feel free to add these if you like. We have included the percussion break in *Lady Madonna* in this collection, even though we omitted it on the CD, because it works brilliantly in performance – we always include it when we perform the song live as it's a wonderful opportunity to get the audience clapping along!

Ticket To Ride

Words and Music by
John Lennon and Paul McCartney
arr Alexander L'Estrange

3

Penny Lane

Words and Music by
John Lennon and Paul McCartney
arr. Jonathan Rathbone

11

12

19

21

Revolution

Words and Music by
John Lennon and Paul McCartney
arr. Mark Williams

23

24

Day Tripper

Words and Music By
John Lennon and Paul McCartney
arr. Jonathan Rathbone

33

34

Norwegian Wood

Words and Music by
John Lennon and Paul McCartney
arr. Mark Williams

44

Birthday

Words and Music by
John Lennon and Paul McCartney
arr Alexander L'Estrange

48

53

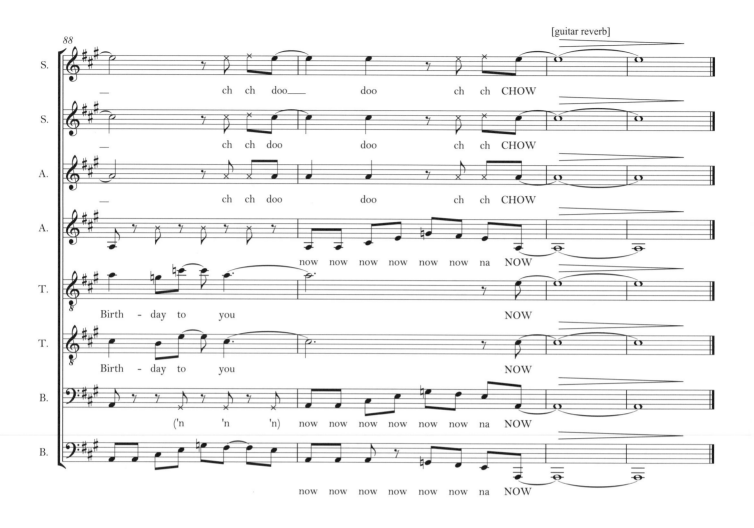

Lady Madonna

Words and Music by
John Lennon and Paul McCartney
arr. Carol Canning

62

Yesterday

Words and Music by
John Lennon and Paul McCartney
arr. Ben Parry originally for Dunedin Consort

64

Strawberry Fields Forever

Words and Music by
John Lennon and Paul McCartney
arr. Andrew Gray

69

repeat and fade

alternative ending

Drive My Car

Words and Music By
John Lennon and Paul McCartney
arr. Simon Lesley

Rhythmically, and with funky cool style

Note: triangular noteheads indicate only the general direction of sound effect pitch, most likely in the extreme of your vocal range.

78

allargando   Slow

S. Ba - by you can drive my car___ and ba - by I love you."___

S. chong chong chong   chong chong   Ba - by you can drive my car___ and ba - by I love you."

A. chong chong chong   chong chong   Ba - by you can drive my car___ and ba - by I love you."

A. Ba - by you can drive my car___ and ba - by I love you."

T. meeb! meeb!   Ba - by you can drive my car___   honk! honk!

T. meeb! meeb!   Ba - by you can drive my car___   honk! honk!

B. bong chong chong chong   chong chong   Ba - by you can drive my car___   ooh

B. Ba - by you can drive my car___   ooh

Blackbird/I Will

Music and Words by
John Lennon and Paul McCartney
arr. Jonathan Rathbone

91

96

When I'm Sixty-Four

Words and Music by
John Lennon and Paul McCartney
arr. Ward Swingle

The Fool on the Hill

Words and Music by
John Lennon and Paul McCartney
arr. Jonathan Rathbone

107

All My Loving

Words and Music by
John Lennon and Paul McCartney
arr. Jonathan Rathbone

I Am The Walrus

Words and Music by
John Lennon and Paul McCartney
arr. Jonathan Rathbone

"Ang" as in French "vin"

Goodnight

Words and Music by
John Lennon and Paul McCartney
arr. Mark Williams

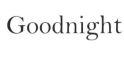

Here, There and Everywhere

Words and Music by
John Lennon and Paul McCartney
arr. Jonathan Rathbone

But to love him is to meet him ev-'ry-where oo

ev - 'ry - where oo ev - 'ry - where

ev - 'ry - where ev - 'ry - where ev - 'ry - where

ev - 'ry - where ev - 'ry - where

ev - 'ry - where ev - 'ry - where ev - 'ry - where

ev - 'ry - where ev - 'ry - where ev - 'ry - where

oo know - ing that love is to share

ev - 'ry - where know - ing that love is to share each one be - liev - ing that love ne - ver dies

know - ing that love is to share each one be - liev - ing that love ne - ver dies

each one be - liev - ing that love ne - ver dies

oo know - ing that love is to share each one be - liev - ing that love ne - ver dies

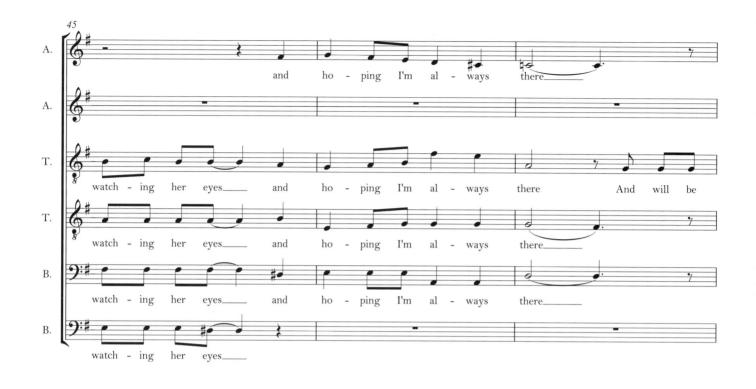

142

OTHER SWINGLE SINGERS ARRANGEMENTS

Many other arrangements by the swingle singers are available in octavo format from several different publishers. All of the arrangements listed below were commercially available in 2003 when this book was published.

1812 Overture	Magnificat
The Agincourt Song	Music History 101
Air on a G String (Bach)	My Lord What a Morning
All the Things You Are	New World Symphony
Amazing Grace	O Come, O Come, Emmanuel
And Is It True?	Organ Fugue BWV 542
The Ash Grove	Organ Fugue BWV 578
Blue Rondo a la Turk	Overture to the Marriage of Figaro
Boars Head Carol	The Oxen
Bouree	Pastime With Good Company
Bushes & Briars	Prelude No. 22
Carol Medley	Quem Pastores Laudavere
Charlie is My Darling	Romance
Clair de Lune	Saints Fugue
Country Dances	Sakkijärven Polka
Coventry Carol	The Sally Gardens
Danny Boy	Silent Night
David of the White Rock	Sleepers Wake
De Punta Y Taco	Soul Bossa Nova
Flight of the Bumblebee	Star of the County Down
Gabriel's Message	Stephen Foster Medley
Gavotte French Suite No.5	Stille Nacht
The Girl from Ipanema	Tre Karleksdikter
Horn Concerto	The Twelve Days of Christmas
How Do I Love Thee?	Un' Aura Amorosa
I'll Be There for You	Un Flambeau, Jeanette, Isabelle
It Was a Lover & His Lass	Vem Kan Segla?
Jingle Bells	Viel Freuden mit sich bringet
Joshua Fought the Battle of Jericho	Waltzing Matilda
The Lady is a Tramp	We Three Kings
Loch Lomond	What Shall We Do With the Drunken Sailor?
Mack the Knife	When I'm 64

All the arrangements listed above are available from Mainely A Cappella, online at **www.a-cappella.com**

PUBLISHERS:

UNC Jazz Press	arts.unco.edu/uncjazz/jazzpress.html
Kikapust Publishing	www.kikapust.com
the swingle singers	www.swinglesingers.com

OTHER A CAPPELLA RESOURCES

MAINELY A CAPPELLA (MAC)

MAC is an online and mail-order catalog and quarterly newsletter. It features more than 3,000 titles, including rare and international releases, more than 1,000 a cappella arrangements and instructional materials. The catalog represents a wide range of styles and genres - from the latest in pop, jazz and world bands to classical ensembles and barbershop harmonies. Mainely A Cappella's electronic newsletter features new releases, pre-releases, and is the only place to find a cappella sale items.

For more information contact:

Mainely A Cappella
PO Box 159
Southwest Harbor, ME 04679
Phone: 1.800.827.2936
International: 1.207.244.7603
Fax: 1.207.244.7613
Email: catalog@a-cappella.com
World Wide Web: www.a-cappella.com
For a FREE catalog call: 1.800.827.2936

VARSITY VOCALS

Varsity Vocals is a student a cappella outreach organization that sponsors four great programs:

- The Best of College A Cappella (BOCA) annual compilation CD encourages college groups to compete for a place on this sought-after CD.
- The International Championship of Collegiate A Cappella (ICCA) brings together hundreds of college a cappella singers who compete in regional concerts across North America for a place in the national finals, held in New York City.
- The Best of High School A Cappella (BOHSA) compilation CD features high school groups from all over the world.
- The Varsity Vocals Summit brings the musical expertise of professional a cappella groups to students, to inspire them to achieve higher musical goals.

For more details see: **www.varsityvocals.com**

ON-LINE COMMUNITY

The Mainely A Cappella catalog has a popular home page on the World Wide Web, at www.a-cappella.com. There are more than 10,000 MP3 sound clips to hear and secure on-line buying. CASA's web site (www.casa.org) has the most extensive online listing of a cappella groups around the globe. There is also a very active newsgroup on the Internet designed exclusively for a cappella fans: rec.music.a-cappella (on the web at groups.google.com). For more specialized email groups, visit groups.yahoo.com and search for a cappella - there are more than 100 ways to interact with fellow a cappella lovers!

THE CONTEMPORARY A CAPPELLA SOCIETY (CASA)

CASA is a non-profit organization formed in 1990 to foster and promote a cappella music. CASA serves both the fan and the performer. CASA members join for three main reasons:

1) To access the extensive CASA arrangement library
2) To receive CASA's bi-monthly newsletter and stay abreast of current topics in a cappella
3) To support the numerous programs CASA volunteers organize for the benefit of the global a cappella community.

CASA programs are produced by a dedicated team of volunteers. They include:

- The A Cappella Summit, which brings hundreds of fans, performers and enthusiasts together for two days of seminars, concerts and workshops
- The Contemporary A Cappella Recording Awards, a yearly quest for the best recorded a cappella music from around the globe
- A Cappella Community Awards, allowing fans to vote for their favorite groups
- The Northern Harmony Canadian a cappella festival and competition
- The A Cappella Almanac, the complete a cappella website with links to all CASA programs and every thing else you might want to know about a cappella
- A Cappella Radio International, a monthly program of music, news and interviews, broadcast internationally and on the World Wide Web
- Tunes to Teens, donating a cappella CDs to middle school kids as an introduction to the world of all-vocal music
- Publications on "Starting an A Cappella Group," "Producing the Ultimate A Cappella Show" and "The Definitive A Cappella Press Kit."

Membership levels begin at $35 a year. For more details please visit **www.casa.org**, or contact CASA:

CASA
PMB 1449
1850 Union Street #4
San Francisco, CA 94123
USA
Phone: 1.415.563.5224
Fax: 1.415.921.2834
Email: casa@casa.org

RETROSPECTIVE

Fugue in D minor (J.S. Bach)
Air (J.S. Bach)
Largo (J.S. Bach)
Badinerie (J.S. Bach)
Eine Kleine Nachtmusik:
Allegro
Romanze
Menuetto
Rondo
En Aranjuez con tu amor
Tango in D major
Romanza Española
Just One of Those Things
Fascinatin' Rhythm
Sinfonia
Solfeggietto
Déjeuner sur l,herbe
(57:31 2003)

Retrospective (UK)

Keyboard Classics (US)

KEYBOARD CLASSICS

Fugue (from the Estro Harmonico,
op.3, no.11)
'C Major Praeludium'
Prelude in F Minor
Clair de Lune
'Moonlight Sonata'
Largo
Golliwog's Cake Walk
Three-Part Invention
Prelude (op.28, no.4 in E Minor)
Gymnopedie No.1
Fugue in D Minor
Rondo alla Turca
Etude (op.25, no.9)
'Harmonious Blacksmith' Variations
Fugue in E Minor
Hungarian Dance No. 5
(42:11 2000)

Keyboard Classics (UK)

RECENT SWINGLE SINGERS DISCOGRAPHY

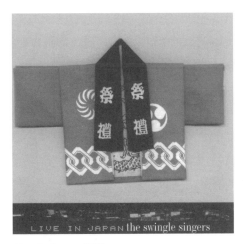

Live in Japan (US)

Live in Japan (UK)

LIVE IN JAPAN

September Song
Alabama Song
Mack the Knife
Someone's Rockin' My Dreamboat
Largo
Badinerie
Air on the G String
Ticket to Ride
A Whiter Shade of Pale
Ave Maria
The Fool on the Hill
Bohemian Rhapsody
Little Drummer Boy
Away in a Manger
Christmas Medley
Amazing Grace
White Christmas
1812 Overture
Thank You
Theme from Mission Impossible
(64:46 2001)

Mood Swings (US)

Mood Swings (UK)

MOOD SWINGS

So What
Surfboard
Insensatez
The Girl from Ipanema
Milonga del Angel
A Timeless Place
What Are You Doing the Rest
of Your Life?
Have You Met Miss Jones?
My Funny Valentine
The Lady is a Tramp
Just One of Those Things
My Foolish Heart
All the Things You Are
It Don't Mean a Thing (If it Ain't Got
That Swing)/Swing Time
Soul Bossa Nova
(61:01 2002)

available from...
The Swingle Singers www.swinglesingers.com
Mainely A Cappella www.a-cappella.com
Selected titles available through U.S. retailers

Ticket To Ride (US)

TICKET TO RIDE

Ticket to Ride
Penny Lane
Revolution
Day Tripper
Norwegian Wood
Birthday
Lady Madonna
Yesterday
Strawberry Fields Forever
Drive My Car
Blackbird/I Will
When I'm Sixty-Four
The Fool on the Hill
All My Loving
I Am the Walrus
Goodnight
(55:36 1999)

Ticket To Ride (UK)

available from...
The Swingle Singers www.swinglesingers.com
Mainely A Cappella www.a-cappella.com
Selected titles available through U.S. retailers